Karate ir

Peter Spanton

Stanley Paul
London Melbourne Auckland Johannesburg

Stanley Paul & Co. Ltd

An imprint of Century Hutchinson Ltd

62–65 Chandos Place, London WC2N 4NW

Century Hutchinson Australia (Pty) Ltd
PO Box 496, 16–22 Church Street, Hawthorn, Melbourne, Victoria 3122

Century Hutchinson New Zealand Limited
PO Box 40–086, Glenfield, Auckland 10

Century Hutchinson South Africa (Pty) Ltd
PO Box 337, Bergvlei 2012, South Africa

First published 1987

Set in 10/12 Monophoto Times

Printed and bound in Great Britain by
Butler & Tanner Ltd, Frome and London

British Library Cataloguing in Publication Data
Spanton, Peter
    Karate in action.
    1. Karate
    I. Title
    796.8′153   GV1114.3

ISBN 0 09 166141 2

Sequence photography: Roy Pell
Still photography: Mike O'Neill

Contents

Foreword

Peter Spanton is a black belt sixth dan in karate-do, the Chief
Instructor of Higashi Karate Kai (Eastern Karate School) and
one of Britain's first black belts. His karate ability is so great
that it prompted one Japanese Master to recommend that he
represent Britain in the kata event at the World Championships.

Previously, Peter fought for Britain at the European Karate
Union Championships, and is a top performer in both kata
and kumite. Not many karateka can claim that distinction.

He was Britain's only world-qualified referee, and for many
years trained our British officials. Having given much time to
national and international karate-do, he now concentrates his
efforts upon training the students within Higashi. So successful
is he that Higashi is regarded as one of Britain's top cham-
pionship performers.

I therefore consider him to be the ideal person to write this
book for young karateka, and have no hesitation in giving it
the blessing of England's national karate governing body.

Dan Bradley
Chairman, English Karate Council
April 1986

Preface

Peter Spanton is one of the finest karate practitioners in the world. You may find that an extravagant statement to make, but as a member of the World and European karate governing bodies I have visited literally thousands of dojos, including many in Japan and Okinawa – the home of karate. In few of them have I found his equal.

Whether it be basics, kata or sparring, he performs each with effortless grace and power. This has come about through his natural coordination, reinforced by decades of constant repetition. This is the key. If you want to shine at karate-do, be prepared to spend time on it.

In this book Peter has set out the basic techniques you must master on your way to the coveted black belt. They are the very cornerstones of your practice, and whether you train for five months or five years you will never outgrow them.

Good training!

David Mitchell
Member of Directing Committee of World Union of Karate-do
Organizations
Member of Directing Committee of European Karate Union

Going the right way

Lunge Punch
Turn
Head Block

Reverse Punch
Turn
Low Block

Front Kick
Turn

Roundhouse Kick

Karate-do means 'The Way of the Empty Hand'. Karate is the fighting system itself, and do is the way it is practised. If you only want to know how to punch and kick then you will learn only karate, but if you want to learn why and how those techniques work then you must delve deeper and study the do.

Many other Japanese martial arts are studied in do forms: ken-do and aiki-do are two examples. It doesn't matter what you practise, as long as you look behind the techniques.

To learn karate-do you must prepare both your mind and body. Do this by setting yourself new targets of endurance when you train. Always try to improve on yesterday's performance.

When you begin training you will want to move quickly to the more glamorous advanced techniques, but the good teacher will make sure you learn your basic techniques first. After all, if you don't get the basic essentials right, how can you build on them?

Some of what you learn may seem pointless to you at the time. Don't worry, the meanings will become clear as you progress through your grades towards the black belt.

11

Training your mind is as important as training your body. Begin by respecting your teachers. They have travelled further than you along the unending way, and have knowledge from which you can benefit. Respect your classmates too – if you can't respect those who like you are studying karate-do, how can you respect yourself?

Don't become overconcerned with winning competitions or gaining your next coloured belt. If you do you will stop following correct training, and suffer either disappointment (when you don't do so well) or conceit (when you do).

Just do your very best and be satisfied with whatever you achieve.

Remember:

1. Always train hard.
2. Always show respect for your teachers and classmates.

This is the only way to study karate-do.

History of karate-do

Since this is a practical book, I don't want to spend too long discussing history. Having said that it is still important for the student to know something about the martial art.

There is no point at which you can say 'Karate-do started there!' Karate-do took a long time to develop into the form we now recognize, though the name was first used by Gichin Funakoshi in the early twentieth century.

Previously, the martial art had been known by other names, such as Ryukyu kempo (Okinawan boxing) and even earlier as To-de (Okinawa hand). It was developed by the warriors and peasants of the island of Okinawa as a form of unarmed combat.

The Japanese overlords ruling Okinawa did not permit any form of the classical martial arts to be practised by the native population, and so training was held in secret until the end of the nineteenth century.

The Japanese military became aware of this underground martial art, and persuaded a number of teachers to give a demonstration. The Okinawans selected the schoolteacher Gichin Funakoshi to be their representative, and he gave a

13

demonstration on the mainland which was attended by the then Crown Prince.

So impressed were the Japanese with Okinawan karate that they encouraged Funakoshi to stay on the mainland and open a training hall. He was soon followed by other Okinawan masters and various schools were established.

Funakoshi continued developing the Okinawan martial art so it could be taught effectively to large numbers of people. To make study more acceptable to Japanese students he named it karate-do, giving it a proper Japanese title.

After the Second World War, karate training resumed in Japan and occupying American servicemen came into contact with it. They in turn introduced it to America. Authentic karate-do was introduced to Britain during the 1950s by the Japanese teacher Mitsusuke Harada. He was followed by other Japanese representing the major styles.

A governing body called the British Karate Control Commission was set up, and this later split into separate groups covering England, Northern Ireland, Wales and Scotland.

Karate-do is recognized by the International Olympic Committee, and in Britain by the British Olympic Association.

The right karate club

I now want to talk about where to learn karate-do. If you already train in a club, then fine; but if you do not, here are some tips that will help you to find the right one.

First of all make sure the club you join is recognized by the English Karate Council. The Council is the governing body for English karate, and trains karateka to represent us in international competitions. By doing this you will guarantee that the training you receive is of a high standard. Otherwise you will have to decide for yourself whether the training is good, and this can be difficult if you are not an expert.

Don't be taken in by fancy looking certificates of competence. The only certificate you need to see is the Martial Arts Commission Coaching Award. This confirms that the coach is both capable and safe. If you train at his/her club you will receive what are called Martial Arts Commission Licences, which include a good insurance policy.

All English Karate Council clubs issue Martial Arts Commission Licences.

The coach will be qualified in two ways. First of all he/she will wear a

15

black belt. There are different standards within the black belt, with first dans being the most junior and eighth dans being the most senior. Dan grade shows how much the instructor knows about karate and how long he/she has been training.

The second qualification to look for is the Coach Certificate. Just because someone is an eighth dan in karate-do doesn't mean they can teach others how to be as good as they are. A coach is someone who is specially trained by the English Karate Council to be able to teach effectively.

Next look at the club to see whether it meets on nights which are suitable for you. Be prepared to travel, especially if you want to train in a particular style (I'll discuss this later). Karate clubs are fairly widespread throughout Britain, especially near the major cities, but in smaller towns and villages your choice will be limited.

The participation fees vary between clubs. Don't think that because you are paying more you will automatically receive a better training. This is not the case. Usually you must pay an annual registration fee with the club of your choice. This fee includes your club membership and your MAC licence. You will also pay mat fees for each training session.

The right training

Don't buy a karate suit before first checking whether your club can supply you. Often clubs keep a stock of suits which are cheaper than the ones you buy from your local sports shop. If you are a beginner, buy the cheapest grade of suit because you may not find karate-do to your long-term liking. After six months you can consider buying a premium-quality suit, but be warned – they are expensive!

Buy the suit a size too big, with plenty of room around the shoulders, hips and bottom. Suits shrink steadily with washing – more quickly if you wash them in very hot water.

A white belt comes with the suit, and this is the correct colour in most clubs for beginners. As you improve you have the chance to take gradings. These are practical examinations where you demonstrate what you have learned. If you pass the grading you will be entitled to swap your belt for one of a different colour. I use the following belt colours in my association:

Beginners	white belt
After three months	white belt
After six months	yellow belt
After nine months	orange belt

After twelve months	green belt
After fifteen months	purple belt
After eighteen months	brown belt
After twenty-one months	brown belt
After twenty–seven months	brown belt
After thirty-three months	black belt first dan

The above timescale is only approximate and based upon the student training twice or three times every week, with regular weekend courses.

Choosing the right style

Because karate-do developed from a number of different schools, it exists today in several styles. No style is any better than another. It is the person who makes the style, not the style which makes the person.

The following are the major styles of karate-do practised in Britain:

Shotokan

This is the largest style practised in Britain. It was introduced into Japan by Gichin Funakoshi, and is named after the place in which he trained.

Shotokan is a very long and graceful style, with lots of katas involving large, powerful movements.

Wado ryu

This was developed from Shotokan by Funakoshi's senior student, Hironori Ohtsuka. The name means 'Way of Peace'.

Wado ryu uses higher stances and whiplash movements during strikes.

Shotokai

This was also developed from Shotokan by a group of Funakoshi's senior students. The name means 'Shoto's Way'.

19

Shotokai is very flowing and generates power through soft-appearing movements.

Goju ryu

Goju ryu was introduced into Japan by the Okinawan, Chojun Miyagi. Its name means 'Hard/Soft School', and this refers to its blend of soft and hard moves.

Goju ryu is very powerful and uses special weights to build up physical power.

Shito ryu

This is pronounced 'Sh'toe Reeyoo'. The style is named after the two teachers who inspired the Okinawan, Kenwa Mabuni, to develop it.

The most popular version practised in Britain is Taniha shitoryu, otherwise known as Shukokai ('Way for All'). Shukokai uses scientific principles applied to karate techniques to develop great power.

Kyokushinkai

'The Way Of Ultimate Truth' style of karate was originated by the Korean, Masutatsu Oyama. He was very interested in the practical applications of karate, and founded his style on those considerations.

Kyokushinkai uses a very vigorous form of sparring called knockdown.

How to find out more about karate styles

Write, enclosing a large stamped, addressed envelope to:

The English Karate Council,
First Floor Broadway House,
15–16 Deptford Broadway,
London SE8 4PE

21

Safe practice

Karate-do is a hectic activity which improves physical fitness in many ways. It places a work demand on the body which you must equal by increasing your fitness. If you suffer from any complaints which might affect your training, then tell the club coach.

If the club coach knows about them, he/she will be able to keep an eye on you.

If you suffer from asthma, take your inhaler and keep it close to hand. Karate training will make you breathless and you must learn to distinguish between this and the onset of an attack. As a matter of fact, karate training is good for the lungs and you may find your condition improving through training.

Diabetics can expect a couple of small problems until they discover how training affects their sugar levels. Keep some lemonade or a quick sugar source close by and dip in when you begin to feel the effect of low sugar. Tell your coach how low sugar normally affects you and he/she may be able to detect symptoms even before you do.

If you suffer from the occasional epileptic fit, don't train in a club with a solid, hard floor. Sprung wooden floors or mats are safer for you. Explain your problem to the coach, and describe any signs which indicate a fit is imminent.

Make certain you get a Martial Arts Commission Licence before you begin training. This will insure you against injury and also cover your partner. Note the date when the licence is due to expire, and apply for a new one in plenty of time by writing to the association registrar.

Start your training with a warm-up programme of exercises. This will gradually raise the activity level of the muscles from that needed in normal everyday work to that needed for karate training. A sudden changeover is less pleasant.

After training it is equally necessary to cool the muscles back down to a normal level of activity. During hard work, the muscles become filled with fluid and this has to be pumped away by gradually lessening muscle action. If you don't do this, aching muscles and stiffness will result.

Start stretching exercises during the warm-up. Karate-do needs quite a lot of suppleness, and a stretching programme is vital to proper training. Stretching is best done slowly, holding the joint at maximum stretch for ten to twenty seconds. Don't jerk or try to use sudden bodyweight to load the stretch, otherwise something can tear.

23

Exercise at least three times a week, and add a spot of running, cycling or swimming to raise your overall fitness level. The object of this kind of training is to make you fit enough to concentrate on karate technique and not on just lasting through the session.

During training proper, don't jam your arms out absolutely straight as you punch because this can damage the elbow joints. Similarly, don't let your kicks crack out full against the natural limit of the knee. This eventually damages the cartilage and ligaments.

Making a fist

When you mention karate-do to people, they immediately think of the karate chop. Funnily enough knife hand (to give it its correct name) is nowhere near as common as the fist. The fist, in one form or another, is the main hand technique of karate-do.

Not many people are able to make an effective fist. This is why they hurt themselves when they try to punch. The first thing you must do is get your fingers out of the way because it is only your knuckles that are supposed to strike the target.

Begin by opening your hand (fig. 1). Roll your fingers down to the top of your palm (fig. 2), then close your fist fully, locking your thumb down across the first two fingers (fig. 3). If you look at a side view of the fist, you will see that the knuckles are well forward and the fingers back out of harm's way (fig. 4).

At first you may not be able to make a good fist and your fingers will poke forwards. Work on this by lightly punching a firm (but not hard) surface. I'll tell you more about making up a practice pad shortly. Alternatively, press your fist against a flat surface.

25

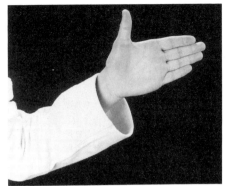

Fig. 1

Fig. 2

If you look at your knuckles, you will see they don't all lie in one straight line and it is impossible to use all of them. In karate-do we use only the knuckles of the first two fingers. This has the effect of concentrating a lot of force over a small area, making the punch more effective.

Don't keep your punch tightly rolled up, because if you do the muscles of

26

Fig. 3

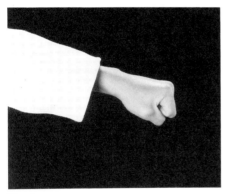

Fig. 4

your forearm will soon tire. Hold the fist firmly, and tighten it fully just as you are about to connect. This will give a slight improvement in power.

Make sure you do tighten both fist and wrist on impact, otherwise you will certainly suffer a painful injury.

We always twist the fist on impact because it gives a further bonus in power. In basic form, this means turning

27

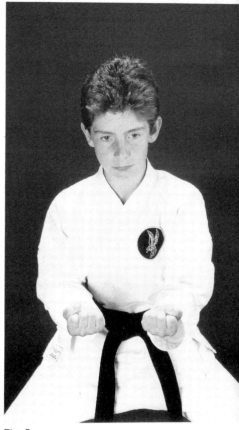

Fig. 5

the fist from a starting position of palm up (fig. 5), to a finishing position of palm down (fig. 6). The fist is turned by a strong twisting action of the forearm.

When you have a good fist, train it by lightly striking a practice pad made from layers of closed cell plastazote foam. This is similar to polystyrene, but

28

Fig. 6

doesn't break up easily. If you use three or four layers, tie them together with a belt and have your partner hold them against his/her shoulder. This will get you used to punching hard against another's body mass. When you are used to the training, get your partner to move about as you punch.

29

Power punching

Power punching makes use of a number of principles. I have already mentioned a few of them in the last section. Now I want to tell you a little more.

Look at the stance (fig. 7). See how the right guard is well forward with the left fist on the hip. Turn your hips slightly away from the front. When you punch, a number of things happen at once.

Firstly push with your left leg and momentarily lift the right foot. This causes a slight forward movement. Don't lift your foot too high or move too far forwards – a couple of inches is enough. Your left leg must remain pressed to the floor when it can act as a prop for the punch.

As weight returns to the front leg, twist your left hip in the direction of movement and then begin to pull back your right arm. Moving at exactly the same rate, your left fist moves off the hip. Don't change the positions of your hands at first.

Quickly picking up speed, your advancing left fist passes the withdrawing right. As the left fist is about to connect – and not an instant before – it turns palm downwards. At exactly the

Fig. 7

same time, your right fist comes to rest on the hip (fig. 8).

So let's look at the sequence of moves once again:

1. Push off the back leg and lift the front foot.
2. Twist the left hip forwards.
3. Pull the front arm back and punch with the left fist.
4. Rotate your forearm and tighten up your wrist and fist as you connect.

Make sure there is no hesitation between the moves; one flows smoothly into the next. As 1. is completing, 2. has begun – and so on.

31

Fig. 8

Why does this sequence make your punch more powerful? Moving forward behind any technique adds body weight to it. Always try to move behind a technique, even if only by a short distance. Twisting your hips into the punch adds the turning power of the body to the strength of the arm. Pulling back the lead hand causes the shoulders to swing, adding upper body power. You already know about twisting and tightening the fist.

Finally, breathing out sharply as you punch will tighten up the muscles of the stomach and make your body more

Fig. 9

rigid and better able to absorb recoil.

A simple way to practise power punching is to stand in a straddle stance and put one fist out, in front of the centre of your own chest. Turn it so the palm is facing downwards. Put the other fist on your hip, and turn it so the palm is facing upwards (fig. 9).

Pull back your leading hand, rotating it as you do. At the same time begin punching with the fist on your hip, but keep the palm facing upwards until just before impact. Try and move both your arms at exactly the same time and speed so they both come to a stop together

33

Fig. 10

(fig. 10). Keep your shoulders square to the front, and don't bring them forward behind each punch.

Start slowly and gradually build up speed. Let your hips move freely and you will see that they tend to move slightly in a whiplash manner behind the stronger, faster punches.

Other hand techniques

There are two other ways to use your fists. Make a normal fist and then strike downwards (or outwards) like a club, landing with the muscle on the little finger side. For obvious reasons, this is called hammer fist.

Hammer fist is a good weapon to use because a band of muscle cushions the bone and protects against bruising. Make sure that you connect with this cushion and not the bones of the wrist! Tighten your fist as you connect.

Hammer fist is often used to deflect attacks, knocking them to one side in what is called a lower parry.

You can also use the upper surface of the knuckles for attacks, especially to the side of the head. This is called back fist. Back fist is not an easy technique to use against a hard target, and it is necessary to train for impact using a practice pad.

If you open out your hand and lock the thumb in across the palm, you have a choice of three techniques. The first is knife hand, which connects in the same way as hammer fist – with the pad of muscle on the little finger edge of the palm.

Be careful not to land on the wrist, or on the little finger joint. Tighten your

hand as you connect, both to prevent the fingers from rattling about and to concentrate power. Keep your thumb tucked in where it can't catch in sleeves.

Knife hand is effective against the throat, or side of the neck. As with the punch, try to rotate your forearm just before impact; this will generate a useful bonus in power.

Ridge hand is less common and uses the thumb-edge of the palm against the throat or neck. Move your thumb well across the palm, and strike with the whole side of the hand in a wide, swinging action. This is a difficult technique and requires a lot of practice on the pad.

Spear hand uses the tips of your fingers against soft parts of the body. As you might expect, it takes a great deal of practice to stiffen the fingers sufficiently to stop them painfully flexing on impact. Some schools slightly bend the middle finger to make it the same length as its two neighbours.

Spear hand is driven into the target and rotates either thumb-upwards, palm-upwards, or palm-downwards as it connects.

36

Using the ball of the foot

The ball of the foot is used for two different kinds of kick, the first of which is called front kick.

The ball of the foot is the pad of flesh on the underside of the foot, beneath the toes. To practise how the foot is held during front kick, stand normally, then raise your heel as far off the floor as possible, keeping the ball of your foot pressed down.

If you raise your heel high enough, your toes will be pressed back and your instep (the upper surface of your foot between toes and ankle) will be in line with your shin. This is the correct foot position to use for front kick.

As with the fist, only the impact area must connect with the target. If you don't pull your toes back, they will connect first and flex painfully. To get maximum power, keep your instep and shin in as close in line as possible (fig. 11). If your ankle is bent it will flex on impact, and not only will you lose power, you may also sprain your ankle.

To hold your foot rigidly in this position all the way through a kick would not be a good idea, because the tightened leg muscles would slow it down.

37

Fig. 11

Therefore practise so you can keep your foot relaxed until the last instant.

The direction the kick travels in is very important, and is influenced by the way you first lift your kicking foot off the floor. Most people push off with the ball of the foot, so the heel rises first (fig. 12). This is a bad fault because then the ball of the foot must be swung upwards to bring it into the target. This movement alone is responsible for many foot injuries because, as often as not, the toes bang painfully into the opponent's forearms or elbow.

The correct way is to push with the heel, so the foot lifts horizontally

Fig. 12

(fig. 13). By doing this the foot is correctly angled for use, and can be driven straight into the target with minimum risk of injury.

Never kick up into the target for the reasons mentioned above. Bring your kicking knee to the correct height, so it is pointing at the target before releasing the kick. If you do this, it will travel straight.

Bend your knee and keep the lower leg vertical – don't let it swing outwards or you will leave your groin open to attack.

When you raise your knee, keep your upper body relaxed and maintain an

Fig. 13

effective guard. Make sure you don't hunch your shoulders up, since this will make the kick jerky. Standing on one leg makes you vulnerable to attack, so keep your arms close to your body where they can protect you.

Roundhouse kick also uses the ball of the foot, but in a different way to the last technique. Stand normally with feet flat to the floor, then pull back the toes on your kicking leg. This is the foot position for roundhouse kick.

You may find this slightly easier to do than the front kick position, but actually it is as difficult. Pulling the toes back in this position takes a greater effort.

40

The foot is in a normal position, and it is more difficult to make the ankle rigid so the foot may flap about.

As with front kick, lift your foot straight off the floor. Don't push off with the ball of the foot or it will be more difficult to pull the foot into a correct position. Keep your foot relaxed until it is about to connect, then tighten the muscles up.

Bring your kicking knee to the correct height before you kick. A good round-house kick demands that the foot swings horizontally, or even drops slightly into the target. If you don't raise your knee enough when kicking to a high target, it will travel diagonally upwards and catch your partner's elbow or shoulder.

Roundhouse kick uses a lot of hip twist, so there is a marked tendency for the arms to fly around. Watch this care-fully – use a mirror if one is available – and check to see you are keeping an effective guard.

41

Using the instep

The instep is another part of the foot used in karate-do. This part of the foot is not so well cushioned as the ball of the foot, and consequently it is used against softer targets such as the groin or face.

The actual part which connects is the upper surface of the foot near the ankle. If you land hard with the part nearest the toes your foot can bend back painfully, so get the range right.

To get the foot position, point your foot until it is in line with the shin. Curl your toes downwards so the upper part of your foot is stretched and the ankle stiffened. As I have mentioned before, don't keep your foot tensed up during the kick, just tighten it as you are about to connect. Don't allow it to flap about though, or injury can result.

When using the instep, lift your heel off the floor first. This gets the foot immediately into the correct position. Then lift your kicking knee to the correct height and make the kick.

Because careless use of this technique can cause you injury, only use it when there is an actual target; don't just throw the kick and hope it will hit something.

Using the heel

Like the ball of the foot, the heel is well padded. It is used in a variety of kicks which mainly rely on a thrusting action to make them connect hard.

To get the foot position, stand normally and roll your foot outwards, so weight presses on the outer (little toe side) of the foot edge. Once your foot is like that, try and lift your big toe on its own whilst curling down the other four toes. Some people find this easy; for others it is more difficult – though everyone can do it after a little practice.

Whilst you are learning the toe position, it is acceptable if you lift or curl down all the toes together.

The reason for this awkward sounding foot position is to give the foot an edge by rolling the heel out. In a little while you will find you can take up the foot position quite quickly.

Don't use the kick like a club, because if your aim is off you can connect with the edge of the foot instead of the heel. This isn't so bad when lightly attacking the opponent's ribs (as with a snap side kick), but it can cause a painful sprain if you don't land correctly with a thrusting kick.

Because the foot is held unnaturally, a great deal of muscular effort is needed

43

to hold it firmly. Therefore learn how to tense your foot quickly from a relaxed position, presenting the heel first to the target (fig. 14).

To help get your foot into the correct position from the outset, don't raise your heel as you lift it from the floor.

Since kicks using the heel are mainly straight thrusts, so it is even more important that you get your kicking knee to the correct height. When side thrust kicking to the opponent's head or upper body, you will have to lean back.

Fig. 14

This is acceptable, but do keep your back straight and your head lifted.

The heel is driven in a straight line into the target using a lot of muscle power. The hip rotates behind the thrust kick, so the full length of the leg is used. During hip rotation you are open to counterattack, so make sure you keep an effective guard.

Because a lot of hip twist is used during side and back thrust kicks, the ball of your foot will drop lower than the heel. This is very noticeable in back thrust kick, where your foot points almost down to the floor. If this happens, it shows your foot position is correct. Make sure, however, that the heel never drops below the level of the toes.

Using the inside edge of your foot

The inside edge of the foot lies on the big toe side. To get your foot into the correct position, do the same as you did for the heel kicks mentioned in the previous section. Roll your foot onto its outside edge and lift the big toe, pressing the other toes downwards.

Although the foot position looks the same, the technique is applied differently. The sole of the foot, with inside edge leading slightly, scoops as it contacts and either knocks the opponent's technique to one side, or catches the ankle in a technique known as foot sweep.

Since the legs carry the weight of the body, any successful attempt to jar or hook them will need a lot of power and a rigid ankle. If you foot sweep with a relaxed ankle, you are certain to injure it.

Use the inner edge of your foot to sweep an opponent's guard out of the way by pointing your foot directly upwards, so it stands a better chance of hitting the target.

Don't swing your techniques too widely and with too much uncontrolled force, because if they miss, you may be left spinning like a top!

46

Successful kicking

If you are close enough to punch someone, don't use a kick. Standing on one leg is not a particularly stable stance. Use kicks for longer-range sparring and even then, only against a target.

Many people get injured because they kick when there is no target to aim for. As a result, they smash their feet into elbows, shoulders, hips or shins with painful results.

If you can't quite get your feet into the correct shape, don't try a kick, otherwise a fracture/sprain could result. Always keep a sensible guard and don't push your face forwards.

Power kicking

Kicks are very powerful because the leg is heavy and when travelling fast has a lot of energy. The disadvantage is that they are slower in use than hand techniques.

Karate kicks are powered by a combination of actions. The first comes from the muscles of the upper leg which swing the bent knee to correct height. The second is the hip action which drives the kicking leg forward into the target. The third is the passive flick (in the case of snap kicks) or powered extension of the lower leg.

47

Snap kicks are so called because the knee joint is kept loose and the lower leg snaps out and back as the upper leg comes to a sudden stop. Although fast and effective against vulnerable targets, this action can be quite punishing on the knee joint. Therefore, don't practise hard snap kicking against the air or very soon your knee joints may give out!

Thrust kicks are powered all the way into the target and rely on hip twist. They may not be as fast as the snap kick variety but are extremely powerful and generally have a long range.

Using your hips not only means more power but also more range. Try facing your partner and lifting your right leg, then stretch out with the foot to reach his/her stomach. Have your partner move back slightly out of range and as you are reaching with your foot, twist outwards on your supporting leg. This turns the kicking hip fowards and can add as much as four inches range to the technique.

The angle through which the supporting leg turns will depend upon the type of kick. For front kick, expect to rotate your hip so the supporting leg turns through ninety degrees. For roundhouse kick, rotate it more than ninety degrees and for side kick, turn it still further.

Some people lean back quite a way as they kick. This may be fine for the roundhouse or side thrust kick, but during front kick I prefer to keep my body weight (but not my face) well forwards and over the kicking leg.

In some styles of karate-do, the hip plays a very large part indeed in kicking. During front kick, the hips are driven forwards by arching the back. In round-house kick, the kicking hip rolls up and over that of the supporting leg.

Whichever method you use, the kick should be recoverable so you can quickly pull it back if it misses. After every kick, pull your kicking foot back away from grasping hands. Following front kick, draw your lower leg straight back as though you were cracking a whip. After side thrust or back kick, pull your knee back to your body before twisting back forwards-facing.

Changing guard before you kick is a good way of twisting the upper body so the hips can follow through.

Kicks which use a step or jump are additionally powerful because considerable body weight is added. Make sure, however, that you begin the kick whilst you are still moving. Once you have stopped, the energy of your moving body is lost.

49

Kiai

I have deliberately steered away from using Japanese terminology in this book, but there is no easy way of explaining Kiai in English. It can be translated as the union of mind and body, this referring to a singleness of purpose, where all the power of the body and mind are directed towards a certain point.

In practical terms, it is expressed in the form of a shout which comes from the diaphragm and not from the upper chest. It is short, sharp, very loud and sounds like '*Eee!*'

Use kiai to concentrate all your power in a particular technique, whether a block, kick or punch. As your muscles tighten on impact, expel air with your diaphragm and shout.

Some karate schools use kiai with every movement, but I prefer to save it for turns in basic technique and for strong attacks in sparring. The use of kiai is very important and it is an essential part of the form of training known as kata.

Standing correctly

If you are wobbling about off balance, you can't do a good technique. Therefore train never to be caught on the wrong foot by using correct stance work.

A stance is simply a way of standing which helps you move quickly in the right direction and/or make a good technique. A correct stance allows you to quickly deal with a situation.

For example, an evasion uses a fast movement in a particular direction, so your stance must be suitable for it. If you are standing on one leg (yes, there is a stance where you stand on one leg – but then only for short periods), you will find it difficult to dash backwards.

Alternatively, if you dig in and meet your opponent's attack without flinching, you will take up a long, low stance that uses the back leg like a prop to prevent you being forced backwards. If you stand too high, you can easily be pushed off balance.

Not all stances are meant for the cut and thrust of fighting. Some are just polite ways of saying 'Hello' or 'Goodbye' to your instructors and classmates.

51

Fig. 15

Polite stances

Polite stances show your teacher that you are ready to be taught. You may, for example, stand upright, with your heels together and feet slightly turned outwards. Your arms hang down at your sides with palms pressing against trouser seams.

This is attention stance, and is so named because it is the one you use when paying attention to the instructor. Say 'Hello', 'Goodbye', or 'Excuse me', without words by facing the instructor or senior grade in attention stance and bowing forwards from the waist.

Don't bow too low or too quickly, otherwise you will look like a penguin! Don't stick your bottom out, and do keep looking at the instructor as you bow (fig. 15).

Don't just bow to the teacher, show respect also to other students. As you enter or leave the training hall, make a habit of pausing and bowing to the class.

From attention stance step a little to the side – first with the left foot, then with the right. If you don't step too far, the outside edges of your feet will end up about a shoulder width apart. Let the arms hang naturally down at your sides and form good fists. This stance says 'Now I'm ready', and is therefore called ready stance.

Before any kind of training, always go from attention stance to ready stance, and when you finish practice, reverse the order.

There's one other polite stance I want to mention. At the beginning and end of training, it is common for everyone to kneel down and make formal bows from that position. To get down into the kneel, drop your right knee to the floor, the left swivelling outwards. Keep your arms pressed to your sides.

As weight settles on the right knee bring the left in and down, then sit back on your haunches with back straight and palms flat on knees. Don't lean in

any direction and don't let your head loll about.

At first this can be difficult to master and your feet may not be able to bend back far enough. With a little practice, however, you will be able to hold a kneeling position for the necessary time.

Practical stances

Stances are made up of three different parts. These are:

a) The length
b) The width
c) The height

When you walk, your front foot is set down in front of the other. This is known as the length of the stance. Attention stance has no length but, because the feet are a shoulder width apart, it is said to have width. The height of a stance depends upon how long or wide the stance is, and how bent the knees are. It refers to the height of the body from the floor.

The first practical stance I want to consider is called forward stance. This is a long stance, with the front foot a good one and a half steps in front of the rear. Don't make the stance so long that your rear heel pulls off the floor. Straighten your back knee and don't let it bend.

Your front leg is bent so the knee lies just above the instep. Don't bend it too little, or too much. Push your knee out-

Fig. 16

wards to brace the stance. Make sure your hips face full to the front (fig. 16).

Test forward stance for width by dropping your rear knee to the floor and measuring the width between it and the front heel. The width is typically equal to two fists, touching at the thumbs. Insufficient width causes a wobbly stance, and too much exposes your groin to attack.

Forward stance is ideal for powerful forward and backward movements.

Reverse punch stance is similar to forward stance. First take up forward

55

Fig. 17

stance, then pull your leading foot back and out a matter of inches, turning it so it points in the same direction as the back foot (fig. 17).

To keep your hips facing the front now needs a little more effort. If your stance is too long when you turn your hips fully to the front, you may find that your rear heel lifts.

When the front foot moves to its new position, remember to push your knee outwards. Many beginners let the knee lean inwards, weakening the stance. Don't turn your front foot inwards too

56

Fig. 18

much or you will make it difficult to advance.

Fighting stance is a very general stance, the object of which is to give your opponent the smallest possible target whilst allowing you the greatest flexibility of action.

To achieve this, weight must be evenly distributed over both feet. Bend the knees equally, and lower your centre of gravity so you are stable (fig. 18) and able to move quickly in any direction. Slightly angle your position so you do not fully face your opponent. It some-

Fig. 19

times helps if you stand slightly to the outside of his/her front foot since this gives you a definite edge when using a technique.

From fighting stance move your body weight back so it comes to lie above the back leg. Your legs are now unequally bent. Turn your back foot outwards and slide the front foot across in front of the rear, turning it to face forward and slightly lifting the front heel from the floor.

Your hips have changed from facing three-quarters-on to completely side-

Fig. 20

ways-on, and the position you now hold is called back stance (fig. 19).

This is useful during defence, where it may be your intention to move back slightly from an attack but not so far as to call for a full step.

From back stance bring your weight fully over the rear leg and draw in your front foot. At the same time turn your hips so they face forwards, and lift the front heel free of the floor (fig. 20).

This short, poised position is known as cat stance. It is sometimes used when a short movement is needed to set up

59

Fig. 21

the correct distance. The front foot rests only lightly on the floor and can quickly be used to kick without the need first to shift body weight.

There are two kinds of straddle stance. One has the feet pointing outwards (fig. 21), and the other has them pointing forwards (fig. 22).

From ready stance step out to the side with each foot and bend your knees so that you sink down. Don't have your feet so far apart that the knees drop inwards, and try to stand so that there is a vertical line down from your knees to your feet.

Fig. 22

Stand with your back absolutely straight and don't stick your bottom out. Push the hips slightly forwards and up and this fault will not occur.

If you take up the stance which has the toes pointing straight ahead (or slightly inwards), you will feel pressure against the knees and there will be a tendency to drop them inwards. Make sure you avoid this. If you try the splayed-feet straddle stance, don't rotate them too far or balance will be weakened.

Straddle stances are often used when responding to two attacks coming from different directions.

Effective guard

What is meant by guard? A guard is simply the way you use your arms, legs and body position to protect yourself. A good guard allows you to effectively use a wide variety of techniques whilst making it difficult for your opponent to reach you.

If you stand in ready stance facing your opponent you have no guard and cannot immediately protect yourself if attacked.

Begin learning about guard by getting your hands and feet in the right positions. If your left leg leads, then also lead with your left arm. Bring it away from the body so there is a right-angle bend at the elbow with the fist carried at roughly shoulder height. Slope your arm so the fist is at the projected midline of your body.

If you hold your lead arm too high, attacks can slip in under it. If you hold it too low, your face is not well guarded. If you don't bring your lead arm across the front of your body you will leave a wide opening for attacks. If you slope your arm too much across your chest, you won't be able to use it quickly.

Don't hold the lead arm out too far from the body because, if you do, you won't be able to punch effectively without wasting time pulling it back. Conversely, don't pull your lead arm back close to your chest because this doesn't give you much space in which to block an attack.

Your right hand is held close to the body, the fist lying just above the knot in your belt. Don't pull it too far back, or it will cease to provide a guard and take too long to use as a punch. On the other hand, don't bring your arm too far across your stomach or you won't be able to use it quickly.

You also lead with the same-side arm as foot in back and cat stances. If you don't, then looking in a mirror will show how open and unguarded you are. Of course, not all techniques have the same foot and arm leading, as in reverse punch, for instance, but this is always for a specific purpose and not as a matter of course.

Straddle stances use the same guard as fighting stance but, because the hips are turned, the rear fist cannot be used as a punch without a major change of stance.

Your guard must be free to change as you move, so if you step forwards from a left-leading stance to a right-leading one your guard should change also. Don't leave this change of guard until the last moment or you could be caught out. Either change to your new guard before you begin moving, or halfway through the movement.

63

Moving around

It is no good taking up a stance and then not moving. In any free-spar situation, both karateka are moving and you must be able to close, open, or maintain distance without falling over your feet or losing guard.

Start from left fighting stance and practise inching forwards on your left foot, bringing up the back leg to maintain stance length. Make sure you do draw up the back foot each time, otherwise your stance will get longer and longer. Remember to keep an effective guard as you move.

When you can do the movement correctly, try it quickly by lifting your front foot slightly and sliding it forward a foot or so, using pressure from the back foot to push it. As the slide stops, quickly draw up your back foot an equal distance.

A more advanced movement uses the same quick slide of the front leg followed by a definite step. As your leading left foot stops moving, swing the right foot forwards and inwards, so it grazes the left foot. Let it travel on past and outwards from the front foot. Change your guard as your feet pass each other. This move allows a quick advance (or retreat), and by stepping well out to the side as you step through you can change your angle to the opponent.

When stepping from fighting stance, change your guard at the outset to take weight off the rear foot, thus allowing it to lift quickly. Bring your leg forward so it passes close by the lead foot and travels on an equal distance.

Keep your height constant by keeping both legs bent. Avoid bobbing up and down and keep your elbows close to your sides. Don't lean forwards with your face stuck out or someone may decide to punch it!

When you step, always move your feet equal distances in front of and to the side of the lead foot. This will ensure that your stance doesn't change in height or width.

To step from cat or back stance, put weight down on the front foot before stepping. Bring the stepping foot in very close so it brushes past the lead foot. This will avoid opening your groin to attack.

Stepping from straddle stance to straddle stance uses a move called scissors stance. There are two forms of scissors stance. To practise the first from right straddle, step past the front of your right foot, so your left calf presses against your right shin. Then carry on past the right leg until you have covered the required amount of ground. Keep your knees bent as you step to avoid bobbing up and down.

65

Use the second type of scissors stance when you want to follow with perhaps a side kick. The latter needs a lot of hip action, and it saves a lot of time if you get your hips into the correct position as you step. This time when you step from right straddle, take your left leg behind the right.

Stepping from forward stance is much the same as from fighting stance, except that your centre of gravity is lower and the movement correspondingly more deliberate. Because the stance is low, the tendency to rise up during the step is greater and must be carefully watched.

Reverse punch stance uses a shallow U step that swings the rear foot forwards and into the front foot before it continues on outwards. This swinging movement is sometimes wrongly transmitted to the shoulders so the body turns slightly during the step. Try and avoid this by restricting the movement to your hips.

Speed of step is important, regardless of the stance you are moving from or into. Your opponent will not wait patiently for you! Practise until you can change stance very quickly. When you become expert, such moves as the scissors step will occur so quickly that you appear to be skipping over the floor.

Finally, it is not enough simply to be able to move forwards. You must practise changing from stance to stance as you move backwards and during evasion.

Turning quickly

You must be able to change direction quickly to meet a challenge. There are two principal ways to turn, the first used when you want to turn completely about-face and the second when you want to turn through ninety degrees or so.

The first way uses the rear foot, and I can best illustrate it by reference to left fighting stance. Take up your stance and begin the turn by looking over your shoulder to ensure the coast is clear. Avoid the mistake some beginners make of turning blind.

If it is clear, begin to turn by stepping across with the back foot. Move your foot an equal distance across and to the other side of your leading foot. If you don't step across sufficiently as you turn, your stance will be too narrow and you will end up wobbling about. If you step too far as you turn, your stance will be too wide and your groin exposed.

Also make sure you don't shorten or lengthen the step. If you step up as well as to the side, the resulting stance will be too short. If you step back as well as across, your stance will become too long.

67

Try to keep the knee of your rear leg slightly bent and springy. This will improve the action of the turn. Lift your rear heel clear of the floor and slide it to its new position. Don't lift it clear of the floor.

The turn action takes place in a smooth sequence of movement. Begin by rotating your hips, and delay turning your upper body until tension begins in the muscles of the back and neck. Then release the upper body which rotates to catch up with the hips. Don't use your shoulders to make the turn work, but rely instead upon your hip action.

As the turn is completing, change your guard in one smooth action. Failure to change guard means you will finish this turn with your left hand and right leg leading.

The second way to turn uses the front foot to set up the new stance. From the same left fighting stance look in the direction you want to finish facing, then step back and to the left with your leading leg. Where you position it will determine the exact angle you face. The further you step back the more you will turn away.

Slide your left foot over the floor until it is in the correct position, and then use your hips to rotate the stance to its new attitude. Change your guard as you turn.

Practise both ways of turning from different stances.

68

Blocks

Karate-do isn't just a way of attacking, it is also a means of defending yourself. When someone tries to punch or kick you, you must prevent injury by nullifying the technique.

You can nullify any attack in two ways. The first involves simply moving out of its path. If someone punches to your face with a straight jab, just move your head a couple of inches to one side or the other. This will cause the attack to miss.

The trick is to move the right way when avoiding an attack. For example, you can step back a little from a face punch, only to find the attacker leans a little more forward. You can step to the side of another face punch only to find you have stepped into the curling path of a hook.

The only way to move in exactly the right direction is to identify the attacking technique at a very early stage and select the correct avoidance. This is very difficult, and unless you are skilled you will make many mistakes.

For this reason, it is always best to reinforce your avoidance with a block. A block is simply a way of using the body or a limb to deflect attack.

To be as safe as possible the block you use should cover the maximum

69

area, both in width and in length. If the attack is aimed at your chest, your block must sweep right across the area to be sure of stopping it. The further from your body you block, the more chance of success you have. If you leave it until the last couple of centimetres to block an attack, you are leaving precious little margin for safety.

As with avoidance, you must select the correct block to match the attack. If the attacker aims at your head, it is no use selecting a block that covers the lower part of your body. It would be convenient if there was just one block effective against all techniques, but unfortunately there isn't and so we have to learn a number of different types.

Timing of the block

The attacker always has the initiative. You react to an attack with a block, but by the time you make your move the attack is already well developed. The most advanced method of blocking is simply to counterattack your opponent as soon as he/she moves, using a fast, long-range response which tries to stop the attack by interrupting its delivery.

This has a lot to recommend it because the earlier you block, the slower the attack is. Attacks start from a stationary position and accelerate through to the expected impact. The longer you leave it, the stronger they become.

70

It takes a great deal of confidence to move into an attack, so many of us prefer to let it develop before using a precise block to not only stop it, but to set up a good counterattack.

If you make the attack miss by means of avoidance, it will quickly slow down as your opponent tries to pull it back in preparation for a second attack. During this time too, the skilled karateka can block and counter with little effort.

I always recommend smaller people faced with a larger opponent to make as much use of distance and timing as possible. A large opponent attacks with a great deal of power and a lighter person, no matter how skilled, runs the risk of severe bruising or worse.

At first, you will learn how to block effectively. Next you will combine your block with an effective counterattack. Finally you must try and bring your block and counterattack so close together that they seem like one technique.

Using deflection

Only a brave (and perhaps foolish) karateka blocks an attack full on. I have come across a number of cases where people tried to direct-block a kick with their forearms and suffered broken bones as a result. A correct block meets the attack at an angle and redirects it.

Let me explain it like this: have your partner gently punch you in the chest. First of all put your hand in front of the

71

target and let the punch slap into your palm. This is a full-on block and is only safe when your partner is punching slowly.

With your partner still punching slowly, tap his/her wrist on the side as the punch approaches you. This will knock the punch off course without fighting against it. Such is the principle of deflection which underlies all effective blocks.

Incidentally, you will find it easier to block your opponent if you slap the wrist rather than the forearm. This is because the principle of leverage says that less force is required as you move towards the end of a long lever (i.e., the arm).

Remember, whichever block you use, don't meet the attack full on!

Head block

I want to describe two types of head block. The first uses one hand, the second two. I prefer one-handed blocks because they leave the other arm free to do something else. Nevertheless, two-handed blocks do have certain advantages which I will discuss later.

Practise a head block from a forward stance, and begin by putting your arm into the correct blocking position. Then step forwards (or backwards) quickly and, as the stance is reformed, pull the block downwards whilst at the same time driving the other arm up.

72

Fig. 23

The blocking arm travels up and across the chest, with the fist turned palm towards the face. Make sure the forearm covers the front of your face as it passes because this way it can protect you if your block is too slow. As the elbow passes your face, strongly turn your forearm so the fist rotates knuckles towards the face. Make this rotation crisp, and use it to lock the block into its final shape (fig. 23).

Note that the blocking arm is slightly inclined, so any downwards travelling strikes are deflected. Note also that the

73

little finger side of the fist is turned upwards. This exposes the muscular part of the forearm to the attack and protects the more delicate bones.

The action of the head block is to bump an attacking face punch upwards.

Double-handed head block is useful because it can trap a downwards-travelling head attack. It also covers the face more efficiently in case your block is slow, or inappropriate. Double-handed head block is also known as X block.

Practise double-handed head block with both open and closed hands. Closed fists make a stronger block, but open hands make it easier to seize the attacking limb afterwards.

Start from forward stance and carry both fists on your hips. Turn both so the palms face upwards. As you step forwards bring both arms up and across your chest, forming an 'X'. Keep both palms turned towards you at this stage.

As they pass your face, begin rotating the forearms, so the little finger sides turn suddenly upward in a sharp movement. Complete the block with arms crossed above and in front of your face.

Mid-section outward block

Mid-section blocks use open and closed fists too. The first one I want to describe is outward block. This is so called because it moves from the centre of the body to the outside. It is a strong block and sweeps a wide area of the body.

74

Fig. 24

Practise it from reverse punch stance, with right foot and left fist forwards. Step forwards into left reverse punch stance and, as you are doing so, fold your left arm back and across your stomach. Your fist is turned knuckles-upwards at this point (fig. 24).

As your stance change completes, bring your left arm up like a windscreen wiper, to sweep across the front of your body. As it comes into line with your left shoulder, strongly rotate your forearm so the thumb turns outwards. Time

Fig. 25

the block so it finishes at the same time as the stance change (fig. 25).

If you block too early, your movement will be jerky. If you block once you have stopped advancing, you will lose the energy of movement. As you sweep the block across your chest, keep your elbow close to the body and hold the blocking forearm at a right angle to the upper arm. To get the angle of the upper arm correct, put your right fist in your left armpit and lower your arm until it squeezes the fist.

Don't waste time blocking past the line of your left shoulder.

Augmented mid-section inner block

This block uses a similar windscreen-wiper action to the previous one except that the right arm swings with the left blocking arm. Both arms moving together generate extra energy and make the block more powerful.

Practise it from left forward stance when stepping forwards or backwards into a new stance. As you step drop both arms to your left hip and, as the step continues, bring both forearms up in a circular movement, concluding when the blocking arm is in line with your left shoulder.

Your right arm comes to rest palm upwards across your stomach, and fist pointing to and close by the left elbow.

Mid-section inner block

This block is so named because it travels from outside the body, inwards. Start from right reverse punch stance and step forwards (or backwards) into a new stance. This time, as you step, your punching arm swings out and wide of the body. Keep the thumb of the fist facing forwards (fig. 26).

As you finish stepping swing your arm across your body, still with thumb leading. As it passes the front of your chest, twist your forearm so the little finger

77

Fig. 26

leads. The block is completed when the fist is in line with your right shoulder (fig. 27).

Don't twist your forearm too early and don't overblock past your shoulder. Try not to lead the block with your fist, but rather keep wrist and elbow in one straight line. Distance the block correctly by using a fist in the armpit – as for outer block.

Knife block

Knife block uses the cutting action of

Fig. 27

the edge of the palm to knock an attack off target. Practise it from cat or back stance, whilst both advancing and retreating.

From left stance (fig. 28), step forwards and extend your left blocking arm straight out in front of you. Turn it palm downwards and keep your thumb tucked in. Your open right hand moves up and across your chest until it is nearly cupping your left ear (fig. 29).

As your step finishes cut across with your right hand, initially leading with

79

Fig. 28

the thumb side, then rotate it little finger forwards. Draw back your left hand strongly, rotating it palm upwards as you do so (fig. 30). The action of the body in turning into its new stance provides additional power.

The blocking forearm must be vertical. It must not lean to either side, forwards or backwards. The elbow must be tight to the body and the fingers of the non-blocking hand must be fully extended. Do not allow the wrist to bend.

80

Fig. 29

Lower blocks

As with head block, there are one- and two-handed varieties of lower block. The two-handed form is an X-block identical to the head block variety, but pushing both forearms downwards into an attacking knee. The force of the rising knee is shed by the sliding action of the forearms.

Don't let your fingers or thumbs stick out or injury is sure to result! Also keep your back straight and don't lead with your chin.

81

Fig. 30

Lower parry is a frequently used lower deflection block employing hammer fist to knock a kick to the side. Start from ready stance and step quickly into right forward stance. As you step extend your left arm straight out and downwards, and bring your bent right arm up so the little finger side of the closed fist touches your left shoulder.

As your step finishes, pull back your left arm strongly and drive the right arm downwards in a curving, punching action. Keep your fist turned palm upwards until the last few centimetres, then strongly twist it palm downwards.

The completed block lies just above and to the outside of your right leg.

Do not block past your front knee and don't lean your face into a possible counter. Make the blocking action crisp, and don't swing your arm like a lump of wood. All the power in this block comes from the action of the hips, the elbow joint and the twisting action of the forearm.

Scooping blocks

Scooping blocks are often used against straight kicks, knocking them to the side and sometimes even catching the ankle. In both types, the blocking forearm encounters the kick at the ankle or lower calf and loops under it.

Both sides of the forearm are used, depending upon the stance.

83

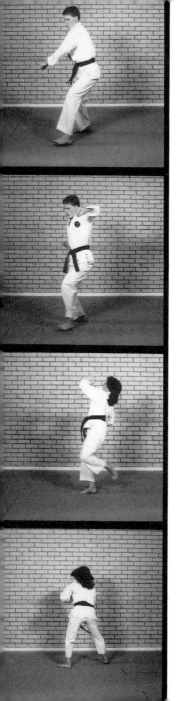

Lunge punch

Lunge punch is one of the first basic techniques you will learn. It teaches coordination, timing and focus.

Begin by stepping into left forward stance from ready stance. Either finish with a left lower parry, or reach forward first with your right arm, then pull it back and punch with the left as your step finishes.

Hold your right fist against the hip, and don't let it move during the step forwards. Step smoothly, keeping both legs well bent so as to avoid bobbing up and down. Step smartly into right stance and, as weight settles on your front foot, pull back your left arm.

Many beginners withdraw their leading arms too soon with the result that they cannot then strengthen the right punch. Time the pull-back so it occurs in the last instants before the new stance is completed. A pull-back too early makes the punch jerky; too late means you can't make use of the energy of the moving body.

As you punch keep your elbows close to your sides and don't lean forwards. Punch to the centre, at about the height of your own solar plexus.

Try a series of lunge punches in succession, watching out for all the faults

I've mentioned. When you run out of space turn into a head block, after first looking over your shoulder, then use the rear foot to step across. Keep your body facing the original way until the last instant, then let it swing around and head block strongly.

85

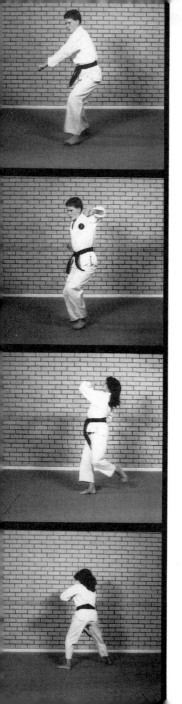

Reverse punch

Begin reverse punch practice from a left forward stance and lower parry, or lunge punch. First punch with your right fist, driving the right hip forwards and pulling back the leading leg. Remember to pull your left fist back strongly, keeping the elbow close to your body. Don't lean forwards.

Step in a semicircle, bringing your right leg up to and past the leading left leg. As you step, your right fist points to the front and must not wag about. As your weight goes forward, pull back the right arm and drive your left hip

Fig. 31

behind the punch. Aim directly in front of your own solar plexus.

Semicircular step is quite slow and you must practise until you can do it smoothly, sliding your foot lightly over the floor. Allow the front foot to turn slightly inwards as you twist the punching hip behind the punch.

Combine reverse punch with a turn and lower parry. First look over your shoulder, then step across with the back leg (fig. 31). Fold your punching arm little finger side against the chest and, as you turn, bring it down and away from your body (fig. 32). Use the twisting action of the hips to provide power.

Finish with your body facing front on in the new direction, and remember to punch first without stepping forward before practising the sequence further.

Fig. 32

Reverse punch/outer block

This technique follows a block with a punch. Begin from left forward stance and left lower parry. Punch without stepping forwards and change to reverse punch stance. Step forward on your right leg and use your right arm for a mid-section outer block, bringing it across your stomach and swinging it out again.

Once the block is completed, immediately pull it back hard to your right hip and punch with the left arm. As your left hip goes forward behind the punch, slightly draw back and turn in your leading foot to correct the stance.

This sequence is a combination of two separate techniques, and each must be performed properly. Don't blur the block into the punch, otherwise it will lack power and form. Time the sequence so you begin the block on the move rather than when you've come to a stop and lost energy.

To practise a turn/block combination, use the sideways foot movement to replace the step in the sequence.

Mid-section inner block reverse punch

As its name implies, this combination sequence links an inner block to a reverse punch. As with the previous sequence, start from left forward stance and change to reverse punch. As you step swing your right arm out to the side, then sweep it across the front of your body, bringing it to an abrupt halt at the correct position. Punch strongly with the left arm, drawing the right arm and hip back.

Don't swing wildly with this block or you will make it ineffective. Hold the block for an instant before punching to preserve good form.

When you turn and inner block, treat the turn as a step forward and swing your punching arm as you swivel your hips. Then bring it across the front of your chest and follow with a punch.

Spear hand

Practise spear hand from a feet splayed straddle stance. Start from left straddle and extend the left arm palm down to the height of the groin. The other remains palm up across the front of the chest.

Twist your left foot forwards and scissors step across the front with the right foot. During this time your hands remain unchanged (fig. 33). Keep your body still as you step but, as the stance change completes, strongly twist your hips and drive your right arm forwards, at the same time withdrawing the left.

You can vary the distance you move each time by experimenting with the length of the scissors step. Do not twist your hips too early, or you will lose a lot of power.

Fig. 33

Front kick

Start from left fighting stance and twist your right hip forwards, putting weight onto the front leg. Change your guard at this time. Pick your right foot up and bring the knee smartly to the correct height. Don't open your groin as you do so.

Swivel on your bent supporting leg and the foot rotates outwards. Keep your arms to your sides as you kick, and relax your shoulders so they don't give a telltale convulsive heave. Kick directly to the projected midline of your own body.

Withdraw the kick as quickly as it went out and set it down gently. If you have kept your weight back over the supporting leg, you will be able to position the spent kick effectively. If weight has gone forwards during the kick, your front foot will slap down hard. This is a bad fault.

Because you changed your guard at the outset, when your kick lands you will be in the correct guard. When you want to turn, look first, then step with your back foot, twisting your body and changing the guard at the same time.

Roundhouse kick

Start from left fighting stance and turn your right hip forwards. Change your guard at this time and keep the elbows close to your sides. Lift your foot straight off the floor and bring the knee up to the side. Quickly turn on your supporting leg so the knee comes around and across the front of your body, then launch the kick itself, striking either with the ball of the foot, or instep.

Don't hinge your body forwards as you kick, but do swivel your supporting leg by at least a right angle. Bring your knee to the correct height and do not kick up in a diagonal manner. Don't swing your knee too far across your body otherwise you may turn too far and land in a vulnerable position.

If you have not leaned forward during the kick your balance ought to be sound, allowing you to put the kicking leg down gently.

93

Side kick

You can practise side kick in two ways.
The first is from a straddle stance. Step
across and behind your leading leg in a
scissors stance. Lean back to maintain
balance, then lift the rear leg up so the
knee comes close to your chest. Turning
your hips away from the direction of
movement, drive your heel out in a
straight line to the target.

Keep your head turned to look at the
target and hold your guard in close to
your body. Provided you have leaned
back far enough, balance will be main-
tained and you can pull your kicking
leg back to your chest before setting it
carefully down in the correct position.

The second way to practise side kick is
from a fighting stance. Keep your arms
close to your sides as you bring your
back leg forwards and up, across the
front of your body. Bring the knee to
the correct height, then drive it into the
target, unrolling your hip in the opposite
direction.

One arm extends along the kicking
leg and the other folds across the front
of your chest. Withdraw your leg simply
by folding the knee back against the
chest, then set it down carefully.

94

Back kick

Back kick is a very powerful kick which, like the previous one, uses the heel in a thrusting motion. In fact, back kick is rather like an extreme form of side kick – one where the hips have turned completely away from the kick's direction.

Start from fighting stance by sliding your front foot across the line of the back foot. Sharply twist your hips so your back faces the direction you want to kick in. Keep your elbows close to your sides as you pick up the rear foot, and bring the kicking knee up close to your body. Drive it out behind you, leading with the heel.

Fig. 34

Fig. 35

Lean away from the kick and keep your head up to maintain balance.

Ensure the kick is on target by stepping across the correct distance. If you step too much or too little, the kick will be off centre (figs. 34 and 35). Twist your hips sharply, and turn completely away before kicking. If you don't turn fully, the kick will again be off target. Pull the spent kick back quickly using a combination of hip twist and knee action. Set your foot down in the correct position or the new stance will either be too wide, or too narrow.

96

Combination techniques

Once you have covered the basic techniques you are ready for what is called combination technique. This is simply a string of basic techniques, one following the other without pause.

The idea behind combination technique is to teach you never to be caught out on the wrong foot. If your reverse punch misses its target, what do you do? Do you give up, withdraw and line up another punch or kick, or do you continue with the attack using other techniques in a logical series of moves?

It is seldom enough to block on its own. If you evade your partner's attack, he/she is unlikely to leave it at that. Therefore after you block, throw a punch or kick. This is the beginning of combination technique.

To get you started, the coach will select combinations. These will not be too difficult or involved at first. Perhaps they will consist of two punches, or a punch followed by a kick. Later, as you become more skilled, you will be able to perform a whole series of punches, kicks and blocks. Ultimately, you will make up and demonstrate your own combinations.

Consider a number of factors when you make up your technique. First of

all, spread the techniques in terms of height and target. If your first attack is to the face, make the second to the chest and so on. This makes the techniques more difficult to block. Secondly, use the hip action of one technique to set up the next. For example, if I am in left fighting stance and punch with my right fist, my weight comes off the back leg and the right hip goes forward. It is then an easy matter to use a right kick.

Alternatively, if I use a high right roundhouse kick to the face and then continue on round, I can use the turning motion to fuel a left back kick to mid-section and, as I continue twisting around to face the front again, I can throw a right reverse punch.

When training in combination techniques don't blur one into the next. Each technique depends on the one before it, so if you start going off balance at the beginning of a series, you will be completely off balance at the end of it. Do each technique properly before going on to the next.

Get the feel of a combination first. Practise it slowly until you can get the correct interplay of movement. Target each technique exactly and, when you feel confident, speed up gradually but never lose the focus of each technique.

Kata

Kata is another of those Japanese words which do not translate exactly into English. A kata is a series of techniques performed in a set manner. They are arranged to teach students how to apply karate techniques.

Originally, kata was the only way in which techniques could be practised. Spear thrusts to the eyes and kicks to the groin are potentially dangerous when used against partners. For this reason, they are not allowed during sparring. Yet these techniques are part of karate-do and should be studied. Kata is the best vehicle for their practice.

Training in kata is good for fitness because certain series are very long and strenuous. Ku shanku, for example, is a very long kata and repeating it a number of times does wonders for your endurance!

The katas Sanchin and Tensho are specially designed to train students in strength and speed. Sanchin holds the muscles of the body in a state of almost constant contraction, making them capable of withstanding hard blows. Tensho shows the other side of the coin and demonstrates that even in apparent softness, there is great strength.

99

At the other end of the scale is the kata Chinto. This uses fast, bird-like movements to evade and counter. Students practising it learn valuable lessons in balance and poise.

Before studying any of these more advanced kata, it is customary to progress through five elementary forms called either Pinans, or Heians, depending upon the school you train in. The Pinans are quite short, with the most elementary being called Pinan (Heian) nidan and the most advanced, Pinan (Heian) godan.

Many beginners find difficulty relating to kata, treating it the same as basic training. They spend a long time learning the movements of a kata, and an even longer time learning the kata itself. This may seem a curious thing to say but at first the student concentrates on remembering the sequence of moves. When these are known, the mind can progress and look for the meaning of that kata.

Some schools explain kata moves by showing their application. This is a very interesting way of learning and helps you visualize what exactly is happening as you practise.

You may practise your kata with the class, or alone. The principle is the same in all cases. Start from attention stance, then when your mind is calm move deliberately to ready stance, and after a moment, begin the kata itself.

The kata is not a race to finish in the shortest time possible. It is a series of connected moves where, for example, you block an imaginary kick, then immediately counter punch – then you pause whilst you look for the next imaginary threat. During the fast sequences, don't blur your techniques into each other. Between sequences have a definite pause, and turn your head to face the new challenge before meeting it. When you finish, remain in your last stance until called back to ready stance by the coach.

The following are the most common katas found in karate:

The Pinans (*Heians*): The five elementary kata.

Ku shanku (*kanku dai*): The longest kata of karate. In the Shotokan style there is another version called Kanku sho.

Nai hanchi (*Tekki*): A curious kata in which the karateka uses a form of straddle stance and moves in a crab-like manner.

Seishan (*Hangetsu*): A powerful kata which mixes slow powerful moves with fast techniques.

Chinto (*Gankaku*): An interesting kata where one-legged stance appears for the first time.

Niseichi (*Niju shiho*): Includes both straight and circular techniques.

101

Passai (*Bassai dai*): A very powerful kata. In the Shotokan style, there is another form called Bassai sho.

Wanshu (*Enpi*): The most advanced kata of the Wado ryu style.

Other popular katas are:

Supar Impei: The longest and most advanced kata of the Goju ryu school.

Tensyo (*Tensho*): A power kata which develops great strength. It stresses loud and forceful breathing.

Gojushiho sho: The first of a series of two strong Shotokan katas using open rather than closed hand techniques.

Unsu: A Shotokan kata using spectacular leaps and sudden drops to the ground.

Seipei: A graceful kata of the Shito ryu style with neat, economical movements.

Sparring

When you become reasonably good at basic and combination techniques, you will be taught how to spar. Sparring allows you to test your ability, aim and distancing in a realistic situation. There are various forms of sparring, the most basic types being one- or three-step.

The club coach may ask your partner to attack you with a specific technique such as lunge punch to the head. He will then tell you to retreat back a step from the punch and deflect it with a head block. If you practise three-step sparring, there will be three lunge punch attacks, one after the other, each meriting a step back and head block.

There are many different possibilities with both punches and kicks. Sometimes the coach will tell you to follow the block with a certain counterattack. This makes you aware of the need for correct timing and distancing.

Since you know what is to happen and your partner knows what you are going to do, the risk of injury is lessened and you can concentrate on getting the techniques right.

Another form of sparring allows the defender to respond in a free way to a set attack. For example, the coach may tell your partner to attack you with front

103

kick. This is all he may use, though he can kick suddenly off either foot. You must respond by countering the kick in any way you wish. This is known as semi-free sparring because although your attacker is restricted in his/her techniques, you are not.

Free sparring is the ultimate development of this progression. Both partners are free to use whatever techniques they want and to both attack and defend freely. There are some safeguards you must watch out for though. Don't kick to your partner's kneecap, or attack his/her face with your fingers open. Don't kick to the shins or groin. Above all, use control to avoid causing injury with any technique.

The body is fairly tough and withstands the odd bump and thump. The face is delicate and doesn't take kindly to being hit. The brain is a delicate organ and too many hard wallops to the head can have long-lasting effects on your state of mind.

Take the sting out of blows by using defensive padding. You can buy fist protectors at the club or from a martial arts shop. These are thin pads of plastic foam which overlie the folded knuckles, yet allow the hand to be opened. Choose ones which have a smooth surface: they won't get so dirty, or scuff your partner's skin. Don't buy the type with padding over the thumb. These prevent you from closing your fist properly.

Shin guards help prevent a scraped shin, but only buy the soft, unbraced variety. They come in two types: one which is an elastic tube and the other which uses Velcro fastening. The tube type is difficult to get on and off and tends to squeeze fatter calves, whilst the Velcro-fastened type often come undone during sparring and must constantly be refixed.

Combined shin and instep guards extend padding over your instep. These are also available in the two types of fixing. When choosing, look at the way they cover the toes. Avoid those which use rubber bands to loop around the toes. These can cause nasty cuts and dislocations. Instead choose those with a broad elastic strap under the sole of the foot.

Groin guards are useful for male karateka, but don't use the removable plastic cup variety which slip into a supporter belt. These can trap any bits and pieces which stray outside, with painful consequences!

Gumshields are very useful, but don't bother with the ones you buy off the shelf. Go to your dentist and have a proper one made. It is more expensive, but it does protect your lips and gums.

Female karateka can either wear a sports bra, or buy one of the commercially made chest protectors.

Don't wear all this equipment throughout the training session. Have it

105

**Outer Block
Reverse Punch**

**Inner Block
Reverse Punch**

**Side Kick
Turn**

Back Kick

close by so you can slip it on quickly when the time comes to spar.

Free sparring should be enjoyable, and you must never let it get out of hand. If you feel you are losing control of the situation and becoming worried, withdraw and bow politely. Then go to the edge of the training area and kneel down.

Karate-do involves an element of combat sport so expect the odd bruise and scrape. Help yourself by taking along a personal first-aid kit in your bag. This should contain paper tissues, crêpe bandages and sticking plasters.

Karate competition

There are two types of karate competition. Sparring competition is a form of free sparring where the object is to score up to a ceiling of three full points in a two- or three-minute bout. There are both male and female individual bouts in weight divisions and team matches consisting usually of five competitors plus two reserves. Mixed bouts between men and women are not allowed.

Bouts are held on an eight-metre matted square. One competitor wears a red belt, the other a white belt. The bout is supervised by a referee, who in turn is assisted by a judge and an arbitrator.

The arbitrator sees that the rules of competition are properly applied by the referee and judge. The referee and judge decide between them which competitor is the winner, or whether there is a draw.

A good technique can score either a full point, or a half point. To get a full point, the technique must be well-nigh perfect. Half points are awarded for slightly imperfect techniques. Sometimes a full point is given for a slightly imperfect technique too, if it was very difficult or highly skilled in application.

Penalties are imposed when either competitor breaks the rules of the competition. When this happens the referee and judge decide whether simply to warn the offender, to allow a half-point or full-point penalty, or to award victory to the opponent. In serious cases, the referee panel may choose to ban the offender from further matches in that tournament.

Penalties accumulate in much the same way that driving endorsements do, and when you reach a certain number in any category of offence you automatically lose the bout.

When the competitors score equally, the referee panel can make a decision based upon their opinions as to which competitor fought better. Where no decision can be made, a draw is given. If a draw is unacceptable and a bout must be decided, then the competitors fight what is called a sudden death extension. The first to score in this extension wins the bout.

The second type of competition is what we call kata competition. The correctness of a performed kata is marked by a panel of five judges, four of whom sit at the corners of the square.

There are male and female individual kata matches and separate male and female team kata matches. In team matches, three competitors perform the same kata in unison.

After the performance of each kata, the judges hold up score cards which show their opinion. Black scores indicate full points, and red scores are decimal parts of the whole numbers. The highest and lowest scores are deleted and the other three added together to form the competitor's score.

If two competitors have the same score, then the lowest points that each scored are added back in. If the tie continues, the highest scores are added back in and, if this too ties, then both competitors have each to perform an additional kata.

There are three rounds in a kata competition. The first round eliminates all but the sixteen best performers. The second round eliminates all but eight, and in the final round the first, second and third places are awarded. If the competition has a low entry, the number of people eliminated in each round may be adjusted.

In some competitions, competitors carry their score through into each succeeding round. This has the advantage of separating out performers and reducing ties.

In the first two rounds, the competitor must choose a kata from an approved list. In the second round, the kata must be different to the first-round choice but still chosen from the list. In the final round, there is a completely free choice and the list need not be consulted. Even katas performed in the first two rounds can be repeated in the third round.

In some styles, there is also a breaking competition. This involves breaking wooden boards with the hands and feet.

SJ4